So I Will
So I Can

Goal Achiever Journal

For Teenagers
And
Young Adults Success

Where there is a will
There is a way
Pursue Your Dream
Discover Your Plan

Benzena Brown

Copyright © 2014 by Benzena Brown

So I Will So I Can Goal Achiever Journal For Teenagers And Young Adults Success
Where there is a will There is a way Pursue your Dream
Discover your Plan
by Benzena Brown

Printed in the United States of America

ISBN 9781628719314

All rights reserved solely by the author. The author guarantees all contents are original and do not infringe upon the legal rights of any other person or work. No part of this book may be reproduced in any form without the permission of the author. The views expressed in this book are not necessarily those of the publisher.

Unless otherwise indicated, Bible quotations are taken from New King James Version (NKJV). Copyright © 1982 by Thomas Nelson, Inc. Used by permission. All rights reserved.

www.xulonpress.com

A person who aims at

Nothing

Is

Sure to get

It

This Journal Belongs To:

Name: _____

Telephone _____

If found, please return

DID YOU KNOW

Excerpt from: Louis Napoleon

?

Research has shown people who use

Goal-Setting

- Suffer less from stress and anxiety
- Concentrate better
- Show more self-confidence
- Perform better
- Are happier and more satisfied

ACKNOWLEDGEMENTS

This journal is dedicated in the memory of my parents, Benjamin Brown Sr. and Clementine Brown. My parents were teachers of love and understanding. I am grateful for my parents teaching. I also must remember my auntie, Mary Slaughter who contributed to teaching me the value of working hard and being consistent, committed, dependable, and honest.

There are many people whom I am indebted who supported me in writing this journal. My family acknowledgements are my granddaughter Rianna Jordan Parker. Rianna, an excellent student and a future leader inspired me when I discovered the limited number of journals for teens. Thank you Rianna. She also provided valuable feedback to making this book an interest to teens and young adults.

My four wonderful children are Benzena Battle, Billy Parker, Damue Bagwell and Camille Bagwell. Billy Parker is my son and photographer. Thank you, young adults; I am pleased you are in my life. My grandchildren are: Rakeem Battle, Neish Battle (artist and assistant) Sabir Bagwell, Sadeja Griffin, Camyra Griffin, Anthony Griffin and Rianna Jordan Parker. I Love you.

My special friend Michael Streeter supported and assisted me in this experience. I am visually impaired and he supported me with transportation as needed. I love you Michael and thank you for your support.

Thanks to my sister Carolyn Perry and my uncle Wardell Langford both of Hampton, Virginia. I love you.

Lorenzo Mills spend hours listening while I worked to make this dream a reality. Lorenzo provided valuable constructive criticism and positive feedback. Thank you my friend.

I, thank Barbara Ellis for giving encouragement and support in the production of this manuscript. I love you Barbara.

The Department of Rehabilitation and Disability (DETR) also was engaged in supporting my dream. My counselor Joy Sprecher-Salander and business consultant Paul E. Watson were motivating and encouraging in making my dream and vision become a reality.

I thank all of my friends for years of their support, fun, and learning experiences. I pray this book will be a life changing experience to all that read it. Remember, if you commit, you will prevail and the secret of success can be found in what you do daily.

I thank God for allowing me to share with you information to discover your plan and pursue your dream in love.

INTRODUCTION

Goal Achiever Instruction Guide

So I Will, So I Can is a goal achiever guide. Lessons are tools and teaching methods to assist in planning, preparing and prospering in your dreams and visions. We all dream. Where there is a will, there is a way to achieve your dream. Goal-Setting has proven results in achievement of goals. The journal lessons include visual aids and power words to aid and prepare you for self-discovery to make your dream a plan of reality. Each lesson consists of an exercise in discovery. Each exercise has thought provoking quotes to enhance your awareness of your visions, dreams and plans. The exercises follow with So I Will, So I Can questions that only you can honestly answer. Apply the quote and the action you are willing to implement to make your dream a reality. Pursue your dream in action, performance and practice. The theory of cause and effect is now in action. A positive energy force is flowing. Remember, you have the authority to change your plans and goals whenever you desire. The motto for life is love is for everyone. Developing a passion of love is creativity in motion, a positive force. Best results for using this journal are with applying the quotes in each section to what you are willing to implement so that you may achieve the results of your goals. Remember, continue to dream big with a step by step process, plan, prepare, profit, prosper.

The Sweet taste of success

GOALS

Golden opportunity at life success- Foundation to prosperous life success

GOLDEN OPPORTUNITY

AT

LIFE SUCCESS

FOUNDATION FOR

PROSPEROUS LIFE SUCCESS

GOALS-GOLDEN OPPORTUNITY AT LIFE SUCCESS

GOALS

Unleash your power

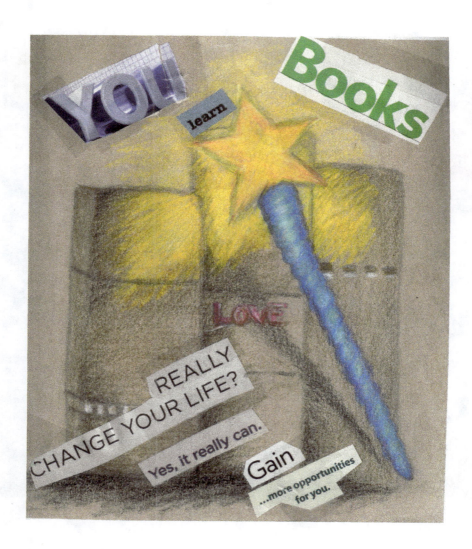

GOALS-GOLDEN OPPORTUNITY AT LIFE SUCCESS

Propel Perseverance and Determination

"SUCCESS COMES IN CANS"

GOALS

Golden opportunity at life success

OPEN

DOOR

T0 >>>

SILVER LINING

Discover your silver lining- you discover your own resilience

(Sweet Taste of success)

GOAL SETTING

*Fear surfaces when you do not know where
you are headed, develop a plan*

So I will

Plan Prepare Profit Prosper

GOAL SETTING

Goal-setting prepares and enable a prosperous deposit of interest in your future

So I Can

Plan Prepare Profit Prosper

GOALS

"Success Comes in Cans" - Louis Napoleon

Daily Goals

Plan Prepare Profit Prosper

GOALS

"Success Comes in Cans" - Louis Napoleon

Weekly Goals

Plan Prepare Profit Prosper

PLAN-PREPARE-PROSPER

GOALS SUPPORT PREDICTIONS

Make it Happen- As a person thinks so he or she is

Big Dreamer!! "I am the greatest!!!" I float like a butterfly and sting like a bee." "I am beautiful!!!" Captivating much attention, he became heavyweight champion of the world. His words brought him attention on television, radio, newspaper and around the globe. Many were in disbelief as he predicted the outcome of his championships. He seemed to believe his words. The power of his words became the foundation to promote his goals. He repeated these words continuously, "I am the greatest." I float like a butterfly and sting like a bee." These words he supported with action.

His name is Muhammad Ali. Mr. Ali is remembered as one of the heavy-weight boxing champions of the world. Additionally, he is also remem-bered for his predictions. His words and action brought him fame.

Many laughed at his words, joked about the victory he proclaimed; how-ever, he did not let their laughter and jokes stop him. "I am the greatest; I am beautiful, too beautiful to be beaten." "I float like a butterfly and sting like a bee!!!" His amazing, victory predictions brought stunning results. People became curious about his next victory and begin to like, imitate and chatter his victory words. "I float like a butterfly and sting like a bee; I am beautiful, too beautiful to be beaten!!!" "I am the greatest!!!" Big dreamer, he expected the best, did his best, and received his best. He is called one of the greatest boxers ever. He is remembered as he proclaimed, "I am the greatest."

Mr. Ali quotes, "What keep me going are my goals." The purpose of goals is to provide positive and useful feedback to you. Be mindful, positive words have positive power. Picture this, negative words produce an effect like a bubble, soon it will pop. Be all you can be, try becoming a goal-setter.

What is a goal and what are the benefits of goals? A goal may be defined as a useful instructional tool or guide with a plan for an expected out-come. Goals set the pace for self-discovery because you are the author and originator of the expected outcome. Start date, action taken, achievement, responsibility, improvement, time management is all controlled by you. Completion or failure to accomplish or meet your goals is controlled by you. It is important to make your goals clear, written, manageable, and achievable with steps designed to complete a successful outcome. Goals are building blocks to the pursuit of happiness. Mr. Ali as we recall states "what keep me going are my goals" Goals are beneficial to achievement when one is focused on a dream, vision or any positive expected outcome.

Dream Big with a step by step guide your goals. Remember, you are the manager, a leader, and author of your goals. Remarkable benefits! Your choices are written, achievable and allows for growth. You too are the greatest, and this not a laughable matter. I applaud you. Take action, begin goal-setting.

GOALS SUPPORT PREDICTIONS

Make it Happen- As a person's thinks so he or she is

Think Possible

GOALS

*"Nothing is impossible, the word itself says
I am possible"-unknown*

So I will

Plan Prepare Profit Prosper

GOALS

*Golden Opportunity at Life Success
is my Goal*

So I Can

Plan Prepare Profit Prosper

Give Thanks

GOALS

Goals Offer Abundance Life Security

GOALS

OFFER

ABUNDANCE

LIFE

SUCCESS

Give Thanks

DAILY AFFIRMATIONS

I give thanks

Today, I give thanks for love, understanding and wisdom

I believe

I Believe I am a winner

I set goals

I set goals with plans to manage, achieve and be open to change

I learn

I learn from my experiences, success and failures

I forgive

I forgive myself and others for any and all misunderstanding

I listen

I recognize listening is good and essential to effective communication, awareness, understanding and observation

I honor

I honor my father and mother

My dreams

I have the ability to live my dream and pursue my dream

Time management

I will manage my time responsibly, allowing time for completion of my goals, study, recreation, rest, family and friends

Plan Prepare Profit Prosper

DAILY AFFIRMATIONS

Every day presents new opportunities

<u>I will remember</u>

- My enthusiasm and joy reflects a positive example

- Big or small my personal victories are keys reminding me that I am victorious

- I see how richly blessed I am and say thank you

- I will pursue my dreams knowing I have the ability to manifest my dreams

- I will remember to ask in order to receive

- I will remember to tap into the power of prayer a power surge

- Prayer changes things

Plan Prepare Profit Prosper

DREAMS

The road where potential meets discovery

Dream Big

DREAMS

*Pursue your dreams-what you do today
is important*

So I Will

Plan Prepare Profit Prosper

DREAMS

Understand Purpose- Dream
Big Visionary

So I Can

Plan Prepare Profit Prosper

if you can DREAM it you can do it

VISION

42

VISION

"If you do what you always did you get what you always got "- Mom Mabley

So I Will

Plan Prepare Profit Prosper

VISION

"When the student is ready, the teacher will appear"-unknown

So I Can

Plan Prepare Profit Prosper

SO I WILL SO I CAN

F.A.N.

Fitness And Nutrition

So I Will

I am my own fan with a healthy lifestyle

F.A.N.

Fitness And Nutrition

So I Can

I am my own fan with a healthy lifestyle

FUTURE OPPORTUNITY KEY

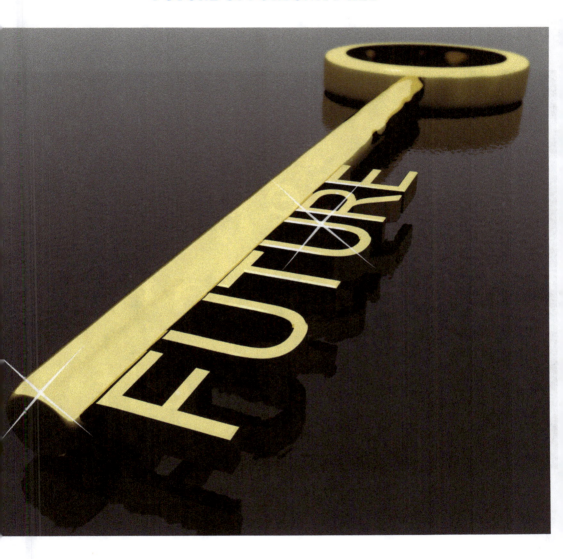

HABITS

HABITS

*To make habit a success, you must practice
habits of success continuously*

So I Will

Plan Prepare Profit Prosper

HABITS

Turn weakness into strengths

So I Can

Plan Prepare Profit Prosper

ATTITUDE

A positive outlook create a winning attitude

So I Will

"As the mind thinks the body will follow" - unknown

ATTITUDE

I have an attitude that reflects my ability to succeed

So I Can

Plan Prepare Profit Prosper

RESILIENCE

Michael Jordan States:

If you are trying to achieve

There will be road blocks

I have had them,

Everybody has had them;

But obstacles do not have to stop you

If you run into a wall,

Don't turn around

And give up

Figure out how to climb it,

Go

Through it or work around it

RESILIENCE

Fear not, be afraid not to try, to try is to discover

RESILIENCE

*Power your passion become
suited for success*

So I Will

"Where there is a will there is a way"- English Proverb

RESILIENCE

*I will remember I am designed to be creative
and victorious, that's unique*

So I Can

The sweet taste of success

SIMPLY CHOICE

Just as there are colors in the rainbow

And the sky is above

And the grass grows from a seed

There are steps to learning

Each step advances to the next step

Each step is a step forward

To your future

You are the cause and effect

Your success is your choice

As steps step forward to learning

Failure is left behind

Recognize the lessons failure bring forth

As I continue to advance my steps in learning

It's SIMPLY CHOICE

SIMPLY CHOICE

Give attention to your actions; breathe life into your dreams, your visions, goals and relationships

So I Will

_____

_____

_____

_____

_____

_____

_____

_____

_____

_____

_____

_____

_____

_____

_____

_____

_____

_____

_____

_____

"Things do not just happen; things are made to happen"
John F. Kennedy

SIMPLY CHOICE

Embrace creativity

So I Can

*Life is a gift of multiplication activated
by love-invest interest*

CHOICES

It depends on you!

BUILDING BLOCKS

I believe in my dreams and know that the doors of opportunity are open

Love and Passion   Honesty   Preparation and Planning
Honor   Prayer   Discipline   Learning   Visions

Time management   Creativity   Study   Gratitude

Service   Awareness   Reading   Recreation   Listening

Positive Attitude   Goals   Positive Habits   Healthy Life
Respect   Dreams   Fitness   Believe Failure

Rest   Family   Friends   Proper hygiene   Appearance

Love   Grooming   Faith

Make it Happen

BUILDING BLOCKS

My imagination is a source of creativity

I am willing to

_____
_____
_____
_____

I am willing to follow

_____
_____
_____
_____

I am willing to improve

_____
_____
_____
_____

I am willing to recognize

_____
_____
_____
_____

BUILDING BLOCKS

*"Things do not just happen; things are
made to happen "John F. Kennedy*

I am willing to begin goal-setting

I enjoy

I manage my time

I act now because action changes things

BUILDING BLOCKS

Recognize where you are

So I Will

I practice constant use of embracing life in a positive thinking active attitude

BUILDING BLOCKS

Honesty is an important asset

So I Can

*My foundation is built to stand and weather
the storms*

STUMBLING BLOCKS

Help is available when you ask

**Peer pressure   Bullying   Opposition   Lack of confidence
Sadness**

**Dishonor   Denial   Rebellion   Excuses   Sorrow
Neglect**

Being untruthful   Stealing   Drugs   Procrastination   Tardiness

Irresponsible   Foul language   Teasing   Jokes that offend

Crimes   Trespassing   Depression   Drama   Stress   Rejection

**Failure   Abuse   Violence   Name calling   Hunger
Lack of nutrition   Frustration**

**Lack of sleep   Restlessness   Fighting   Frequent
Complaints   Disease**

*"The smallest deed is greater than the
largest intention" unknown*

STUMBLING BLOCKS

Help is available when you ask

I am willing to recognize

I manage my time

My habits are having positive results

My choices are considered with thoughts of success

STUMBLING BLOCKS

Remember to be the best you can, what you do now will show up later

So I Will

STUMBLING BLOCKS

I will continue to move forward despite obstacles

So I Can

Obstacles will be placed in my junk file for deletion as I step forward to achieve

IMAGE

Your life is like a lamp that was destined to be placed on a high stand, so the world around you can see it shining - Matthew 5:15

Speak to you

The person I plan to become

The things I plan to do

The things I dream to do

IMAGE

Take a look at yourself

The things I want to have

The things I enjoy most

The things I invest my time in

IMAGE PICTURES

Reflections of a successful, satisfying future I see it today

IMAGE

The reflection in the mirror, is speaking to me

So I Will

Plan Prepare Profit Prosper

IMAGE

Take care of the small stuff

So I Can

Plan Prepare Profit Prosper

RAP TO YOURSELF

"Remember the secret to getting ahead is getting started "Mark Twain

Sample – Get started- Rap

Keep on achieving- um um

Can't stop now

Move up a little higher

To reach my goals

It does make sense

To reach my goals- um um

And discover>>>>>>>> Ain't no stopping me now

Start your Rap

Work in progress-my imagination- create my own lyrics

RAP TO YOURSELF

Melody a tune name success is my choice

So I Will

I name that tune called success

RAP TO YOURSELF

I seek and find solutions to make my dream possible

So I Can

Plan Prepare Profit Prosper

TIME

Time is the beginning of a new day

God has given this day to use as I will

I can waste it or use it for good

What I do today is important

Because

I am exchanging a day of my life for it

When tomorrow comes, this day will be gone

Forever

Leaving in its place something that I have traded for it

I want it to be gain, not loss

Good not evil

Success not regrets

Unknown

Revised

TIME MANAGEMENT

Remember the future begins now-
your plans, goals matter

So I Will

TIME MANAGEMENT

*Time is an important and valuable asset
and must be managed*

So I Can

*Remember the future begins now- your goals
and plans are future investments*

WHAT'S NEXT

FUTURE

*Your goals, dreams, visions is a road map
that lead to your potential future*

So I Will

Plan Prepare Profit Prosper

FUTURE

Start goal-setting now-action changes things

So I Can

Plan Prepare Profit Prosper

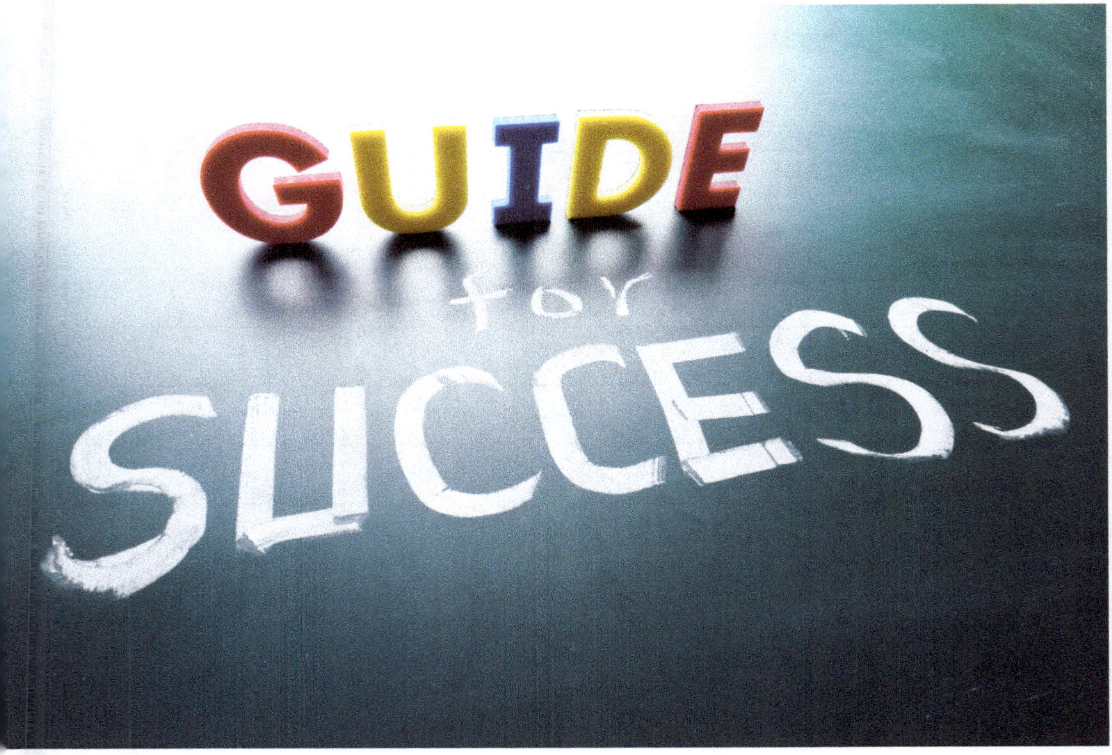
GUIDE
for
SUCCESS

GOAL GUIDE

Goals –Golden Opportunity at Life Success

January

Opportunity

1._____   16._____

2._____   17._____

3._____   18._____

4._____   19._____

5._____   20._____

6._____   21._____

7._____   22._____

8._____   23._____

9._____   24._____

10._____   25._____

11._____   26._____

12._____   27._____

13._____   28._____

14._____   29._____

15._____   30._____

31._____

My imagination reveals to me, ideas for planning and completion of my goals, for this I give thanks

GOAL GUIDE

Goals offer achieving life success

February

Commitment

1._____   15._____

2._____   16._____

3._____   17._____

4._____   18._____

5._____   19._____

6._____   20._____

7._____   21._____

8._____   22._____

9._____   23._____

10._____   24._____

11._____   25._____

12._____   26._____

13._____   27._____

14._____   28._____

29._____

Discipline is the bridge between goals and accomplishment

GOAL GUIDE

Act- Action Changes Things

March

Will Power

1. _____   16. _____
2. _____   17. _____
3. _____   18. _____
4. _____   19. _____
5. _____   20. _____
6. _____   21. _____
7. _____   22. _____
8. _____   23. _____
9. _____   24. _____
10. _____   25. _____
11. _____   26. _____
12. _____   27. _____
13. _____   28. _____
14. _____   29. _____
15. _____   30. _____
                               31. _____

"The secret of getting ahead is getting started "Mark Twain

GOAL GUIDE

"Where there is a will there is a way" English Proverb

April

Health and Exercise

1._____	16._____
2._____	17._____
3._____	18._____
4._____	19._____
5._____	20._____
6._____	21._____
7._____	22._____
8._____	23._____
9._____	24._____
10._____	25._____
11._____	26._____
12._____	27._____
13._____	28._____
14._____	29._____
15._____	30._____

F.A.N. become a fan of your health with proper fitness and nutrition, the body loves this, F.A.N. Fitness and Nutrition

GOAL GUIDE

I recognize the benefits of responsibility, therefore I accept responsibility for my actions

May

Responsibility

1._____   16._____
2._____   17._____
3._____   18._____
4._____   19._____
5._____   20._____
6._____   21._____
7._____   22._____
8._____   23._____
9._____   24._____
10._____   25._____
11._____   26._____
12._____   27._____
13._____   28._____
14._____   29._____
15._____   30._____
31._____

The sky is the limit

GOAL GUIDE

Failure is not a person but an event

June

Resilience

1._____ 16._____
2._____ 17._____
3._____ 18._____
4._____ 19._____
5._____ 20._____
6._____ 21._____
7._____ 22._____
8._____ 23._____
9._____ 24._____
10._____ 25._____
11._____ 26._____
12._____ 27._____
13._____ 28._____
14._____ 29._____
15._____ 30._____

I will advance forward by implementing and applying my goals disciplining myself to succeed

GOAL GUIDE

"It always seem impossible until it is done"- Nelson Mandela

July

<u>Awareness</u>

1._____   16._____

2._____   17._____

3._____   18._____

4._____   19._____

5._____   20._____

6._____   21._____

7._____   22._____

8._____   23._____

9._____   24._____

10._____   25._____

11._____   26._____

12._____   27._____

13._____   28._____

14._____   29._____

15._____   30._____

31._____

Knowledge is power, understanding is development to maturity

GOAL GUIDE

Never give up-victory is ahead

August

Perseverance

Discovery is in failure, you learn another way to achieve your goal

1._____
2._____
3._____
4._____
5._____
6._____
7._____
8._____
9._____
10._____
11._____
12._____
13._____
14._____
15._____

16._____
17._____
18._____
19._____
20._____
21._____
22._____
23._____
24._____
25._____
26._____
27._____
28._____
29._____
30._____
31._____

Key is keep educating you

GOAL GUIDE

*Get clear and gather understanding of your plan,
you create and discover*

September

Wisdom

1._____	16._____
2._____	17._____
3._____	18._____
4._____	19._____
5._____	20._____
6._____	21._____
7._____	22._____
8._____	23._____
9._____	24._____
10._____	25._____
11._____	26._____
12._____	27._____
13._____	28._____
14._____	29._____
15._____	30._____

Wisdom understands motto of life- Love is for everyone

GOAL GUIDE

Strength Is in the heart of things

October

Courage

1._____   16._____

2._____   17._____

3._____   18._____

4._____   19._____

5._____   20._____

6._____   21._____

7._____   22._____

8._____   23._____

9._____   24._____

10._____   25._____

11._____   26._____

12._____   27._____

13._____   28._____

14._____   29._____

15._____   30._____

                                                    31._____

Make a difference- "The smallest deed is greater than the largest intention" unknown

GOAL GUIDE

Knowing is to teach

November

Knowledge

1._____ 16._____

2._____ 17._____

3._____ 18._____

4._____ 19._____

5._____ 20._____

6._____ 21._____

7._____ 22._____

8._____ 23._____

9._____ 24._____

10._____ 25._____

11._____ 26._____

12._____ 27._____

13._____ 28._____

14._____ 29._____

15._____ 30._____

Teaching will make a difference, however it is the instructions that are not always understood

GOAL GUIDE

*Limitations are in words like never and can't
and will cause missed opportunities*

December

Understand

1._____   16._____

2._____   17._____

3._____   18._____

4._____   19._____

5._____   20._____

6._____   21._____

7._____   22._____

8._____   23._____

9._____   24._____

10._____   25._____

11._____   26._____

12._____   27._____

13._____   28._____

14._____   29._____

15._____   30._____

31._____

Develop your understanding and continuous seek knowledge

SUCCESS ACHIEVEMENT GUIDE

The benefits of goal-setting are clear, personal and achievable

January

1._____   16._____
2._____   17._____
3._____   18._____
4._____   19._____
5._____   20._____
6._____   21._____
7._____   22._____
8._____   23._____
9._____   24._____
10._____   25._____
11._____   26._____
12._____   27._____
13._____   28._____
14._____   29._____
15._____   30._____
                              31._____

Plan Prepare Profit Prosper

SUCCESS ACHIEVEMENT GUIDE

The benefits of goal-setting are clear, personal and achievable

February

1._____

2._____

3._____

4._____

5._____

6._____

7._____

8._____

9._____

10._____

11._____

12._____

13._____

14._____

15._____

16._____

17._____

18._____

19._____

20._____

21._____

22._____

23._____

24._____

25._____

26._____

27._____

28._____

29._____

Plan Prepare Profit Prosper

SUCCESS ACHIEVEMENT GUIDE

The benefits of goal-setting are clear, personal and achievable

March

1._____   16._____
2._____   17._____
3._____   18._____
4._____   19._____
5._____   20._____
6._____   21._____
7._____   22._____
8._____   23._____
9._____   24._____
10._____   25._____
11._____   26._____
12._____   27._____
13._____   28._____
14._____   29._____
15._____   30._____
                              31._____

Plan Prepare Profit Prosper

SUCCESS ACHIEVEMENT GUIDE

The benefits of goal-setting are clear, personal and achievable

April

1. _____
2. _____
3. _____
4. _____
5. _____
6. _____
7. _____
8. _____
9. _____
10. _____
11. _____
12. _____
13. _____
14. _____
15. _____
16. _____
17. _____
18. _____
19. _____
20. _____
21. _____
22. _____
23. _____
24. _____
25. _____
26. _____
27. _____
28. _____
29. _____
30. _____

Plan Prepare Profit Prosper

SUCCESS ACHIEVEMENT GUIDE

The benefits of goal-setting are clear, personal and achievable

May

1.
2.
3.
4.
5.
6.
7.
8.
9.
10.
11.
12.
13.
14.
15.

16.
17.
18.
19.
20.
21.
22.
23.
24.
25.
26.
27.
28.
29.
30.
31.

Plan Prepare Profit Prosper

SUCCESS ACHIEVEMENT GUIDE

The benefits of goal-setting are clear, personal and achievable

June

1._____
2._____
3._____
4._____
5._____
6._____
7._____
8._____
9._____
10._____
11._____
12._____
13._____
14._____
15._____

16._____
17._____
18._____
19._____
20._____
21._____
22._____
23._____
24._____
25._____
26._____
27._____
28._____
29._____
30._____

Plan Prepare Profit Prosper

SUCCESS ACHIEVEMENT GUIDE

The benefits of goal-setting are clear, personal and achievable

July

1._____
2._____
3._____
4._____
5._____
6._____
7._____
8._____
9._____
10._____
11._____
12._____
13._____
14._____
15._____

16._____
17._____
18._____
19._____
20._____
21._____
22._____
23._____
24._____
25._____
26._____
27._____
28._____
29._____
30._____
31._____

Plan Prepare Profit Prosper

SUCCESS ACHIEVEMENT GUIDE

The benefits of goal-setting are clear, personal and achievable

August

1. _____
2. _____
3. _____
4. _____
5. _____
6. _____
7. _____
8. _____
9. _____
10. _____
11. _____
12. _____
13. _____
14. _____
15. _____

16. _____
17. _____
18. _____
19. _____
20. _____
21. _____
22. _____
23. _____
24. _____
25. _____
26. _____
27. _____
28. _____
29. _____
30. _____
31. _____

Plan Prepare Profit Prosper

SUCCESS ACHIEVEMENT GUIDE

The benefits of goal-setting are clear, personal and achievable

September

1._____
2._____
3._____
4._____
5._____
6._____
7._____
8._____
9._____
10._____
11._____
12._____
13._____
14._____
15._____
16._____
17._____
18._____
19._____
20._____
21._____
22._____
23._____
24._____
25._____
26._____
27._____
28._____
29._____
30._____

Plan Prepare Profit Prosper

SUCCESS ACHIEVEMENT GUIDE

The benefits of goal –setting are clear, personal and achievable

October

1. _____
2. _____
3. _____
4. _____
5. _____
6. _____
7. _____
8. _____
9. _____
10. _____
11. _____
12. _____
13. _____
14. _____
15. _____

16. _____
17. _____
18. _____
19. _____
20. _____
21. _____
22. _____
23. _____
24. _____
25. _____
26. _____
27. _____
28. _____
29. _____
30. _____
31. _____

Plan Prepare Profit Prosper

SUCCESS ACHIEVEMENT GUIDE

The benefits of goal-setting are clear, personal and achievable

November

1._____ 16._____

2._____ 17._____

3._____ 18._____

4._____ 19._____

5._____ 20._____

6._____ 21._____

7._____ 22._____

8._____ 23._____

9._____ 24._____

10._____ 25._____

11._____ 26._____

12._____ 27._____

13._____ 28._____

14._____ 29._____

15._____ 30._____

Plan Prepare Profit Prosper

SUCCESS ACHIEVEMENT GUIDE

The benefits of goal-setting are clear, personal and achievable

December

1._____ 16._____

2._____ 17._____

3._____ 18._____

4._____ 19._____

5._____ 20._____

6._____ 21._____

7._____ 22._____

8._____ 23._____

9._____ 24._____

10._____ 25._____

11._____ 26._____

12._____ 27._____

13._____ 28._____

14._____ 29._____

15._____ 30._____

31._____

Plan Prepare Profit Prosper

SO I WILL SO I CAN

Golden Opportunity at Life Success

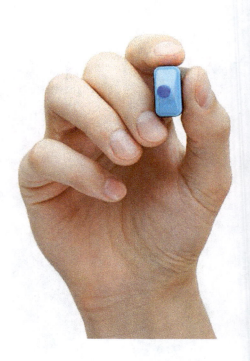

MY SUCCESS STORY

MY SUCCESS STORY

MY SUCCESS STORY

MY SUCCESS STORY

MY SUCCESS STORY

MY SUCCESS STORY

PURSUE YOUR DREAM

(Life)

L OVE

I S

F OR

E VERYONE

GOALS-FOUNDATION FOR

PROSPEROUS LIFE

SUCCESS

FUTURE

Find ur treasure u reach extraordinary

FIND

UR

TREASURE

U

REACH

EXTRAORDINARY

Goals- Golden Opportunity Road to Success

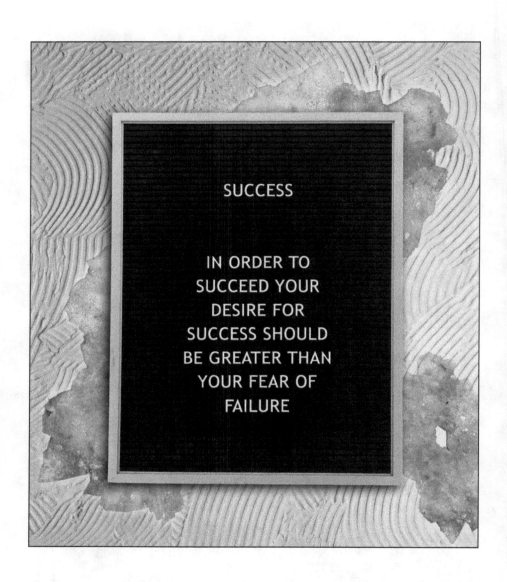

MY AHA MOMENTS NOTES

Discover your Plan

MY AHA MOMENTS NOTES

Discover your Plan

POST AHA MOMENTS NOTES

Discover your Plan

PURPOSE

I am not a fan
of finding purpose
I am a fan of
living with purpose

Jon Acuff

Printed in the USA
CPSIA information can be obtained
at www.ICGtesting.com
LVHW021059191023
761545LV00001B/3